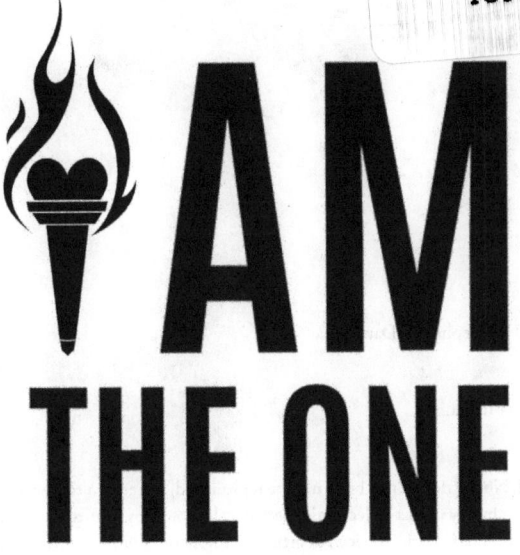

Copyright © 2022 by Stephen A. Davis

Published by Kudu Publishing

All rights reserved. No portion of this book may be reproduced, stored in a retrieval system, or transmitted in any form or by any means—electronic, mechanical, photocopy, recording, scanning, or other—except for brief quotations in critical reviews or articles, without prior written permission of the author.

Scripture quotations marked NKJV are taken from the New King James Version®. Copyright © 1982 by Thomas Nelson. Used by permission. All rights reserved.

For foreign and subsidiary rights, contact the author.

Cover design by: Ebbony E. Doty
Cover photo by: Danny Kang Austin

ISBN: 978-1-957369-51-8   1 2 3 4 5 6 7 8 9 10

Printed in the United States of America

I AM THE ONE

BY STEPHEN A. DAVIS

KUDU

DEDICATION

First, I have to thank God for giving me the opportunity to share with you what He put in me long ago—I Am the One!

To my wife, Michelle Darlene Davis, thank you for always LOVING, believing, encouraging, and praying for me as I continue to carry out my God-given assignment. I love you dearly.

To my daughters, Sasha, Amber, and April, whom I love so much: thank you for your support and inspiration that help me make others great and continue a life-long legacy of wisdom, honor, and empowerment.

To the entire Refresh Family Church and Refresh Nation—a great people who have great potential: may this book unearth your inner potential for immediate results and long-term success.

Thank you to all of those who have worked to make sure this inspirational book was released to the world. My mission is to make people great, and I am certain to carry on this legacy from my late spiritual father. THANK YOU!

ALSO BY STEPHEN A. DAVIS

10 Years of Unprecedented Peace, Favor & Abundance

Words to Inspire You to Dream

CONTACT INFORMATION

Email: info@directconnectinc.org

Website: www.StephenADavis.org

Facebook: @BishopStephenADavis

Instagram: @BishopStephenDavis

Mailing Address:
Refresh Family Church
117 12th Ct NW, Birmingham, AL 35215

Contents

Introduction 9

CHAPTER 1. **What Level are You on Right Now?** 11

CHAPTER 2. **Born with Purpose** 19

CHAPTER 3. **Standing in the Gap** 29

CHAPTER 4. **I Am the One** 37

CHAPTER 5. **I Knew You** 45

CHAPTER 6. **No Excuses** 55

CHAPTER 7. **God, I Need Your Help!** 65

CHAPTER 8. **Find Your Inner Strength** 73

CHAPTER 9. **Genetically, I Am the One** 83

CHAPTER 10. **Test, Conspiracy, Pressure: You are the One** 93

CHAPTER 11. **I AM** 105

INTRODUCTION

Welcome to an experience that will prove to be rewarding and life-altering. This book will unearth your inner potential for immediate results and long-term success. With great confidence and assurance, I'm convinced that this book will touch every class of people, every culture, and all nations.

As a writer, my objective is to stimulate your God-given abilities for the advancement of people around the world. Standing in a faith that is unwavering, I believe your best life is ahead of you and that, without fail, you will experience it. You also will find the strength to believe that you were purposed to be on the earth for this time and for this generation. I'm sure that you are not a "placeholder," as my late spiritual father would say. No longer will you merely occupy a space or have people place things on you until a seemingly better fit comes along.

As you read these pages, courage will begin to invade your heart and mind until fear is slowly eradicated. Like a roaring NASCAR race with a driver waiting for the wave of the green flag, let's GO and fulfill destiny.

You Are The One!

– 1 –

WHAT LEVEL ARE YOU ON RIGHT NOW?

And David left his supplies in the hand of the supply keeper, ran to the army, and came and greeted his brothers. Then as he talked with them, there was the champion, the Philistine of Gath, Goliath by name, coming up from the armies of the Philistines; and he spoke according to the same words. So David heard them. And all the men of Israel, when they saw the man, fled from him and were dreadfully afraid. So the men of Israel said, "Have you seen this man who has come up? Surely he has come up to defy Israel; and it shall be that the man who kills him the king will enrich with great riches, will give him his daughter, and give his father's house exemption from taxes in Israel." Then David spoke to the men who stood by him, saying, "What shall be done for the man who kills this Philistine and takes away the reproach from Israel? For who is this uncircumcised Philistine, that he should defy the armies of the living God?"

(1 Samuel 17:22-26)

There are people who will achieve either personal, family, community, statewide, national, or even global victory. So when we read about David in this passage, there is a national enemy confronting them and David is about to achieve a national victory. Some of you are facing a victory—whether on a personal, statewide, or national level. What level are you on right now? You have to understand where you are. You will go through these processes; once you go through a national victory, there is a possibility of global victory that impacts everything. David, in this particular Scripture, was about to achieve a national victory. Everybody nationwide was going to know about it. No matter David's age, he was about to achieve it!

You should never be afraid of what you have to face or the threats on your way to achieving victory. David had the faith to overcome fear. As he was on his way to deliver his brothers' lunch, he overheard the threat from the enemy, which heightened his faith. It was a personal insult to him that activated his faith to know that he would have the victory. You too must consider that any threat against you is an answer. It may be a personal insult, but allow your faith to be incited to overcome the threat and achieve victory. Anything that you take personally, you have the wherewithal inside to gain victory over—if you have faith! If there is an assault on your community, you have the ability inside of you. You would not have a passion for it if you did not have strength on the inside of you to bring some resolve to that particular problem. The personal attachment you have towards a thing is a sign that you have the answer or the power within to bring a solution to it.

PROBLEMS ARE TIED TO WEALTH

David had a passion for the assault on his people. He felt deeply about it, and then he heard about the rewards for achieving victory: enriched with great riches, given the daughter of the king, and exemption from taxes. Every threat or problem is tied to wealth. Sometimes, when you are running from a problem, you are running from your wealth. Problems and challenges always have an attachment—and it is wealth! If you solve the problem, you gain wealth. If you run from it, you will always struggle in that particular area. Therefore, a problem presents an opportunity to gain wealth. David's family was in poverty and he was just an "ordinary" young man going about his own business. When this problem arose, others fled in fear, but it aroused David's faith. It was not that he was crazy or even outside of the box in his thinking. It was not that something was wrong with him—rather, something was right. The reason you are aroused when you hear a problem is because there is something right with you. You should be stimulated when you hear about a problem, because you should be thinking, "I am the solution." Do not think of yourself as the problem but as the solution. If you believe you are the problem, then believe that you will be "a problem" to what has been a problem...You are the solution, and you must start thinking this way about it! There are three ways to transform your thinking concerning problems. They will stop you from running away from the keys that will unlock wealth in your life and bring about the covenant that you need on the next level very quickly. In one moment, everything can change for you.

> The personal attachment you have towards a thing is a sign that you have the answer or the power within to bring a solution to it.

1) Your faith may seem unusual, but it will be beneficial.
David's faith was unusual, but it was beneficial. Whatever you may be moving into—whether it be your family, community, state, or nation—your faith is going to be unusual. Faith is not the norm; when you walk in levels of faith, it is going to be unusual. We see in this passage that David was walking in another dimension of faith and it was unusual, especially when others were running away afraid. He asked where the threat or the problem was so that he could solve it. Solving that problem was going to be beneficial to him, the army, the nation, and the king. You do not necessarily have to be the king in order to be the problem-solver. David was not the king (at this point), but he was anointed to be the problem-solver. Transform your thinking concerning problems. Use your faith.

2) Faith will bring distinction—you will be set apart.
The type of faith David had brought distinction to his life. He was set apart from everybody else. You have to be able to handle the fact that your faith will set you apart. You are moving and believing and you have a different attitude about everything than those around you. When people wonder why you are so happy, you can tell them it is because you are the answer and you can solve the problem. Faith will bring distinction: you cannot sit in a crowd and *not* be seen. You cannot be amongst people and *not* be noticed. You bring this energy and synergy to the room, to the group, the community, to the nation. Your faith brings a distinction and sets you apart. Get used to it, because you cannot hide when you have this kind of faith. Remember, faith produces and changes the environment in which you are meant to be a problem-solver. Transform your thinking concerning problems, and let your faith set you apart.

3) Be ready for a life filled with results.
When you see this kind of faith and experience it as David did, you need to be ready for a life filled with results—and not just a one-time result. You are not just going to kill the lion or the bear; you are not going to just get victory over the Goliaths you face; you are going to have victory after victory. When you have this type of faith—when you move like David was moving—you are going to have a life filled with results. You need results, and so does everyone else. You have been positioned right now, reading this book, because you are the type of person who is going to believe what you have received. Therefore, you are going to get results. Do not think this is impossible, because with God all things are possible (Luke 1:37). Today, you are going to start to embark upon a life journey that is filled with results by using your faith on every problem that is in your sphere of influence. Use your faith on everything in your environment— when you do so, you are going to be distinct. You will be noticed as that person who not only believes but who gets results. This is the season that you are going to get major results, because you are going to start thinking differently. When you hear a challenge, you are going to challenge it back! Transform your thinking concerning problems and get results.

WHAT ABOUT THE REPROACH?

David began to talk about the reproach or the thing that discredits. You are representing yourself, your family, or whatever group you may be a part of in this situation. It does not have to be a church group. Whatever group you are representing, if anything tries to discredit that group, rise up. Let this sink in: you can only remove that reproach when you have faith—when you believe. What is it that is trying to discredit or bring a reproach in your life? There may even be some things that have been going on generationally to bring reproach; but it is time...you are the one! If you have been trying to figure out who is going to help, who is going to bring forth the breakthrough, it is you! You are going to bring the breakthrough in every single area that you were looking for somebody else.

Look in the mirror. You are the one who is anointed; you are the one called; you are the one reading this book; you are the one gaining influence! Why would you think God would increase your influence if you were not the one? Stop refusing to sit in the room and remain hidden. Instead, let everyone in that room know that you are the one. I dare you to write it down: "I Am the One"! It does not matter where you are in life. David was in poverty, did not have tax exemption, did not have a spouse, was not rich . . . but when he showed up, he was the one! It does not matter what status you currently have or what obstacle you may be dealing with right now. You will be the one in your family, community, state, country, your world. Why are you looking for another? Your faith has positioned you for such a time as this.

You did not show up to the meeting too late—you showed up right on time to hear about the threat. You have heard alarming information. This threat has caused something to rise up in you and make you better. Read the attachment—for every problem, there is an attachment. Anytime it comes from God, and you are the problem-solver, there is wealth, covenant, vitality, and governmental support to those who are the answer. Again, I stress that there is governmental support to those who are the answer. You are the one!

PRAYER

Father, You knew the problems that would arise and You knew what we would be facing. Yet You called us to arise and not to abort the assignment. We will fully embrace what You have called us to do and will complete it. I decree and declare that there is no one else that can do what they have been called to do; no one else can fill the void like they can; no one else can reach people like they can; nor bring down that giant. No one else has the faith they have for that particular project. All Israel believed because David believed and got results. Father, thank You for a belief system that infects entire houses and communities. Thank You for faith and for the results that bring national and international recognition. They are no longer in a box or hidden, but at the forefront. Father, thank You for doing what You said You would do through men and women. Therefore, Your people are stepping out and doing what You called them to do with power and clarity in carrying out the assignment. In Jesus' name, Amen!

Now, tell somebody, *I Am the One!*

NOTES

_____
_____
_____
_____
_____
_____
_____
_____
_____
_____
_____

— 2 —

BORN WITH PURPOSE

On January 25th, we celebrate the life of my mother, Charles M. Davis, who would have been 96 on her birthday in 2022. We thank God for her being born. If she had not been born, I could not have existed, nor my eleven siblings . . . I am the twelfth child. I am the child of government, the child of foundation—born with purpose. I thank God that she saw fit to bring me into this world even in her old age, when the doctors told her she did not need a child. But God needed me in the earth! She was a very great woman, a very gracious woman who was quiet but had a whole lot of presence. My mom was always loving and kind. We never witnessed anything like hate or jealousy demonstrated in our household. We always saw her show generosity and love, a spirit of forgiveness even when she was mistreated. She demonstrated how to extend love and forgiveness and hope to people who did not do everything just right. We saw this in our mother and then we imitated . . .

» How graciously she walked.
» How forgiving she was to others.
» How considerate and extremely unselfish she was, always prioritizing those around her.

I honor my mom, her impact on my life and the people who knew her. She did not talk a lot, but she had a major expression in how she handled people and situations. We never knew the burden that she carried being a single parent in a single-parent household; we never saw the stress on her shoulders. Still, she never stopped believing: that change would come, that things would get better. She was excited to see the positive—even the potential of what could be positive. That is exactly who she was. I wanted to make sure to dedicate this section to her and publicly continue to honor her on January 25th. Everyone was born with purpose.

ARE YOU THE COMING ONE?

> *And John, calling two of his disciples to him, sent them to Jesus, saying, "Are You the Coming One, or do we look for another?" When the men had come to Him, they said, "John the Baptist has sent us to You, saying, 'Are You the Coming One, or do we look for another?'"*
> (Luke 7:19-20)

In these verses, John is digressing. He has to decrease so that Jesus can increase. Therefore, John is moving off the scene at the same time Jesus is entering the platform. I started with this particular Scripture to help you better understand what to expect and where you are in this season. John calls two of his disciples to him and sends them to Jesus to ask, "Are you the Coming One, or do we look for another?" In the previous chapter, I started talking about the phrase, "I Am the One." I am the one to help you better understand that *you* are the one for certain levels of influence. You are the one, and yet you are waiting on someone else to step up.

You are the one who should be embracing the moment, whether it be in your family, your community, state, your nation, or globally. Because John is leaving the scene, he wants to know before he leaves if Jesus is the one. "Are you the Coming One, or do we look for another? I want to solidify and settle it right now that you are the one."

You are no longer going to have an identity crisis; you are no longer going to endure any type of turbulence in relation to knowing that you are the one. Because you are the one, you must learn what particular area God placed you in this earth to impact. Sometimes, we fail because we are trying to impact an area we are not called to impact. But there is an area for everyone. There is an area in which you are the one—and no one else can do what you are called to do. Again, John was asking, "Are you the One?"

AN ANSWER AND A SOLUTION

John sends his disciples, qualified men, to ask Jesus this question. They knew that an answer and a solution were coming, but they wanted, *needed* to know, because it was a little bit difficult. I need to know—are you the coming one? Some of you are thinking, *How can I be the one? Look at where I am, look at the condition I am in right now—it is a bit difficult. Look at the things I am going through.* I want to make this announcement: it did not destroy you. Why? Because you are the one!

> Because you are the one, you must learn what particular area God placed you in this earth to impact.

---

1) Jesus is our example, as well as our Savior and King.
The problem with the church is that they believe Jesus can do things but they cannot do things. That is a major problem, because Jesus said in John 14:12, "Most assuredly, I say to you, he who believes in Me, the works that I do he will do also; and greater works than these he will do, because I go to My Father." So Jesus tells the disciples—and us through

them—that they are going to do greater works than His. I do not know where we dropped the ball thinking that Jesus is always up on this pedestal as a King—and He *is* King. His name is more powerful than any name in the earth; but His name, when used by us, also gives us the ability to do some powerful things in the earth. Jesus is our example of how to operate in power and dominion. If we use Him as an example, as a model, then we'll operate as He did, and greater. If Jesus is your true model—not just your Savior and King, but the example of how you should walk, how you should dominate in the earth—then you are the one, because Jesus is the one!

Embrace the fact that you are the one on whatever level God has called you to operate. Now it is your turn to be an example and bring full strength in the body and to the people who are looking for you. You are the one, whether you be a father, mother, son, or daughter—whether you are in school or college, working a job or operating as an entrepreneur, whether you are in politics, arts and entertainment ... whatever you may be engaged in, you are the one. Jesus was the example John was asking about... "Are you the coming one?" And the answer to that was *yes*!

2) The results will prove that you are the one.
Many of you reading this book may think more about what you have been through than where you are going. Well, what you are going through is proof of where you are going. No one could have made it through what you made it through, nor endured what you have endured, and remained sane. This is speaking to the fact that you were able to process and make it through, and now you are moving. If you are not on the other side, you are moving closer to it. It did not make you quit. You are still together.

Anything that has value has to go through a proving process. The proving process is not always the signs, wonders, and miracles that Jesus did, but there is nonetheless a proving process. Before Jesus performed signs, wonders, and miracles, He was tempted by the devil. He was in the wilderness. He was hungry. He was challenged to throw Himself off of the pinnacle of the temple. He was challenged in worship by Satan and all he represents so that He could obtain the Kingdom. Jesus went through this entire proving process because He was the one.

I want to make an announcement, because some of you think that, because you have been going through things, you are not the one. What you have been going through is the *proof* that you are the one. If you were not the one, you would not have been tested like Jesus had been tested! I realized that I am the one, so I know I had to be tested so that God could use me on the level that He uses me now. How God is going to use you will determine the level or pressure of testing that you go through. You are the one! You are not dead; it did not kill you. You did not commit suicide. You did not throw the towel in completely. You may have had your hand up to throw in the towel, but you did not. They may have been some of the worst days you have ever experienced, but guess what? You had another day. You may as well get positive information in exchange for the turbulent days you have been through.

Some of you know you have been tested in this area: how are you going to love people who are unlovable? This is a test to prove that you are the one. Can you love the people who hate you or the people who have become your opposing enemies? When you are liberated on the inside, you know you are the one. What your opposers did to you—what happened around you—does not change that fact. It reinforces it! Your troubles, challenges, oppositions—all of those things speak to who you are. The challenges show you that you are the one! Everything you have been through, everything that you have experienced, everything that was seemingly distasteful, was an announcement that you are the one.

3) They will have to look no further.
John sent the message, "Are you the Coming One, or do we look for another?" You need to write this down: "You do not have to look any further. I Am the One." Embrace that fact. You have survived. You have survived COVID-19. You have survived all the criticism, all the trauma, all the adjustments, all the heartache. You survived all the brokenness of heart that you experienced on your journey. You are the one—you survived!

This does not mean that you have done everything right, but you did not die. You did not quit. You always knew that something was going to get better at some point because you are the one. Even on your worst day, you knew there would be a better day. Worst days are an announcement that the better days are coming. Many of you experienced COVID-19, a deadly virus, and are still here after over 800,000 people are gone … do you want to know why? Because you are the one.

> Results that have been produced from your life, in spite of all the opposition, prove that you are still standing strong.

I AM THE ONE

I still have my mind. I still have my strength. I still have love for God. I still have love for people. I am the one, you are the one, and that is why God has called you and anointed you. You are their example. Never let Jesus just be your Savior and King. Let Him be your *example* of what you are going to do in this earth. Do not ever forget that you have already proven, through your survival, that you are the one. What you have gone through has solidified the fact that you are the one, and they do not have to look any further. There is no replacement for you. There is no model or substitute for you. There is no one else who can do what you have been designed and proven to be able to do. So if they look over you, the problem is with them, not you. It means that the scales have not fallen from their eyes. Jesus told John's disciples that all they needed to do—and all we need to do—is "look at what I Am doing," and then look at the results. Results that have been produced from your life, in spite of all the opposition, prove that you are still standing strong.

PRAYER

Father, we bless and honor You. Thank You for taking us through the process of pressure and for putting us in place for such a time as this. We will begin to attract things to us from the North, South, East, and West. We attract favor, resources—everything that is needed for those who understand that they are the ones. God, we embrace our identity and we will never let it go again. We will confess it on a daily basis, even when it may be the worst day of our lives—that we are the ones. In the name of Jesus, we are fortified! Amen.

NOTES

_____

_____

_____

_____

— 3 —

STANDING IN THE GAP

So I sought for a man among them who would make a wall, and stand in the gap before Me on behalf of the land, that I should not destroy it; but I found no one.
(Ezekiel 22:30)

Ezekiel was a prophet, and in this passage, he was prophesying that you are the one God was seeking. If He was seeking anyone, He is seeking you. You are the one. Sometimes, we exclude ourselves, but I learned how to include myself. I am the one that He is seeking. You are the one that He is seeking.

Many people who are being sought out by God have spent most of their time in the shadows. You are no longer in the shadows. Do you want to know why God sought for a man or woman among the people? You are amongst so many other people—you are part of a family who would still make a wall and stand in the gap "before me, on behalf of the land, that I should not destroy it, but I found no one." God has to look no further. Just put your hand up. It is you. You are the one! Say to yourself, "I Am the One. I am the one that came from such-and-such family; I am the one that came from such-and-such community; I am the one that came from such-and-such university or school; from such-and-such country."

You are the one with your hand up, suggesting yourself because God is seeking. He continuously seeks every single day; He is looking for not just one person but someone who represents different lands, different bloodlines. He is seeking someone.

GOD IS SEEKING YOU

I do not know how many people are in your family, but He is seeking one out of your family nonetheless. I do not know how many people are in your workplace, but He is seeking one. I hope that what you are reading registers in you because you are the one. You may not understand everything—and a lot of times, it is not about how much you understand but how much you can identify with what is being said. You begin to identify with some things, whether you be in ministry, business, politics, education, arts and entertainment... it does not matter. You are identifying with something I am saying, so this is an announcement that you are the one. In this verse of scripture, God is speaking through Ezekiel who is saying that he sought for a man among them (Ezekiel 22:30a). A lot of times, we can feel like we are lost. Some of us even choose to hide amongst others; but you are no longer in hiding. You are the one because God wants to make a wall. He wants someone to stand in the gap on behalf of the land. God does not want to allow destruction, but He needs someone to stand up. God does not want to destroy anything. He needs someone like yourself to stand up and be accounted for and stay in the battle. It does not matter your background, it does not matter your past. You want to be the one that God no longer has to look any further for because He has found you. Step up and say, "God, I Am the One." Here are a few specific points about the seeking God does for those who will stand in the gap.

1) God seeks for one among many.
God seeks for one among many. It has always been His way of doing things. God is the same yesterday, today, and forever (Hebrews 13:8). Even if you apply this scenario in a corporate arena, businesspeople are looking for one individual. They will hire five or six people, but you must understand that they are only seeking one. So your performance, your attitude, your posture is everything. Know this: they are only seeking one person out of the five or six that they hire.

So what if there are several businesses that open up at the same time as your business? Your business can still trump every other business. You must realize that what you have is more powerful than anything else around you. You are not competing—you are setting the bar. Everybody is going to want to rise to your standard. Be conscious of the fact that you are not trying to be equal or competitive with anyone who is doing what you are doing. You are setting the bar.

Say to yourself right now, "If I am the one, I set the bar."

In Daniel 2, you'll find that Daniel stands out from among the others because the king is looking for someone to interpret his dream. Daniel stands out because he is the one. He has the interpretation. In Genesis 41, Pharaoh has a dream that cannot be interpreted . . . and in comes Joseph. He is the one—he has the interpretation—he has to answer. If you embrace that you are the one, I believe you will have the knowledge and the wisdom that is needed in order to move your organization or structure forward, which is going to change the trajectory of your life. Daniel and Joseph stood out. You stand out. Regardless of the level on which you are operating, you operate on the highest level within your arena. Because you are the one, you set that bar. Set it high, so other people can matriculate up to that standard.

> **If you embrace that you are the one, I believe you will have the knowledge and the wisdom that is needed in order to move your organization or structure forward, which is going to change the trajectory of your life.**

2) God is seeking for someone to fill the gap.
A gap is some area that is broken or open. It is an area that is not closed, as in the case of a wall with a breach. There are a lot of open walls that are full of gaps. There are a lot of breaks in places that have not been filled. You are the one who is going to fill that gap, breach, or broken place. What may have been a threat is no longer a threat, because you just filled that gap! God is seeking for someone to fill the gap. You are the one. God found you, and you are going to fill the gap so that there will be no more breaches. They will not exist because you are there standing up. As we just saw, Daniel filled a gap and Joseph did, too! So can you.

3) God can sustain the land with you.
The land is going to be sustained as long as you are in place. It does not matter how many threats are coming against your household or your organization; if you are in place, you are the one to sustain it. When you are filling that gap, do not lose your place or get disoriented—not now. This is not the time to be questioning whether you are the one who is supposed to close the gap. Just as we read about Daniel being in place with the king and his ability to stop something bad from happening, you too can stop bad things from happening when you are in place.

Understand that God put you where you are for a reason. God is placing and calling you for a reason. You are the one. I cannot emphasize this any more than I am doing right now. Something on the inside of you continuously speaks to the fact that you are the one. Yes, you may be afraid; yes, you may be nervous or feel like you do not know if it can be you . . . You may have even said, "I do not have any examples in my bloodline for what I am doing right now." But *you are the one!*

Catch this: it was not that Ezekiel's prophecy came about because there were any examples in the bloodline, either—it was simply that God had a plan. His prophecy said that someone would rise up and fill that gap, and that was a promise. God said, "Somebody is going to come and close this breach where people have been suffering." I've made up my mind that I am going to say "yes" to God. No matter how I feel, if I am prepared, adequate . . . no matter what, I resolved to say "yes." I'll make sure that there are no more breaches in this particular area. This is how I responded and how you should, too. I hope I am initiating a different thought pattern for you so that you can start moving into those breaches and gaps in your own life. If you are starting to think this way, then know that God can sustain the earth with you.

CALL YOURSELF A GAP KEEPER

A gap keeper can easily be identified in a family when he or she transitions or passes away. All of a sudden, the assets in that group seem to be depleted. This is because the person who transitioned was a gap keeper; they were the ones who closed things up and kept things safe. If you are called to keep things safe, you are also called to bring things to a higher level. I use this statement to describe it best: "In a world of mediocrity, a small amount of excellence makes you stand out in a crowd." You are the one. You can bring things up to a higher level . . . or bring them down. I know you are choosing today to bring things up, especially in a world filled with mediocrity and gaps.

There are a lot of inconsistencies in the world, but as a senior leader and CEO, I show up— whether on the radio, social media, or in person. Why? Because I am closing the gap. You are a gap filler. You are the one who closes the breach. Say, "I Am the One."

PRAYER

Father God, stir up the belief of those who are reading this so that they truly believe that they are the ones called to fill the gap. Give them downloads that cause them to rise up and say, "I Am the One." Amen!

NOTES

– 4 –

I AM THE ONE

So Jesse called Abinadab, and made him pass before Samuel. And he said, "Neither has the Lord chosen this one." Then Jesse made Shammah pass by. And he said, "Neither has the Lord chosen this one." Thus Jesse made seven of his sons pass before Samuel. And Samuel said to Jesse, "The Lord has not chosen these." And Samuel said to Jesse, "Are all the young men here?" Then he said, "There remains yet the youngest, and there he is, keeping the sheep." And Samuel said to Jesse, "Send and bring him. For we will not sit down till he comes here." So he sent and brought him in. Now he was ruddy, with bright eyes, and good-looking. And the Lord said, "Arise, anoint him; for this is the one!"
(1 Samuel 16:8-12)

I AM THE ONE

In previous chapters, we have discussed the fact that you are the one. There are many places in scripture in which God selects individuals. In these verses, we see many came to the prophet Samuel who were in the House of Jesse. Seven sons came by, and yet none of them was the one. The one who was called was out in the field taking care of the sheep. I am going to go through three things next, because I believe we really need to consider the fact that, whether you were in the room or not, you are the one.

1) You were not considered, but you are the one.
Jesse had eight sons, and seven of them walked before the prophet Samuel. The Spirit of God that was upon Samuel did not signal him to choose any of the seven. But neither Jesse nor the other seven brothers even considered the fact it might be David, who was out taking care of the sheep. I do not know about you, but there have been times I was not even considered, and yet I ended up being the one.

You might not have been considered either, but you are the one. You cannot allow doubt in your mind because of how others are treating you or being treated themselves. Just because you were not selected for the job, the promotion, the trip—whatever it may be—does not negate the fact that you are the one.

2) It took time for the others to pass by.
Some of you are battling in the time in which others are passing by. You may think to yourself, "Why is this taking so long?" Well, there had to be seven

sons to walk by the prophet before they realized that the one supposed to be anointed was still working in the field. It took time for one brother to the next to pass by. They went through all the sons. Finally, after the last son, Samuel asked, "Now, is there anybody else?" Perhaps you're reading this and you haven't even come through the line to see if you qualify. Those doing the selecting do not know that you are the one because you haven't had your turn yet.

I want to tell you prophetically that you are coming into your turn. It took time for seven individuals to walk by. The Spirit of God said to each, "No, this is not the one." He was not rejecting them; He simply had already made His selection before they started coming through the line. You may have been selected a long time ago, even though nobody knew it. Now, you have come into an arena in which you understand that you have been selected.

There are messengers in the earth that move by God and not emotions—those individuals are going to select you. Prophets see and think futuristically. They project the future. Samuel had the ability to see who was going to be the future king. He knew there was going to be a king from the House of Jesse, he just did not know which son. I believe that, on this round, when you pass by, this selection is going to be sure.

3) No one will sit or rest until you are in place.
Samuel said to Jesse and his sons, "We will not sit down until he comes here." The posture of sitting is a posture of rest. Because you are the one, no one is going to rest until you are in place. People have been trying to rest; systems have been trying to rest; organizations have been trying to rest, but they cannot until you are in place.

When David got into the house, the word of the Lord came to Samuel and said, "Arise, anoint him; for this is the one." The power of God, the influence of God, knows the one. Many of us who are walking through the earth as Samuel did are anointed by God—we are looking, sensing, and gauging things constantly. We know when something comes by us that God has selected. God saw eight sons and selected one to be king.

Let me reiterate this: you cannot become depressed about the length of time that it takes for others to pass through. You must not get discouraged simply because you were not considered. There are many instances in which God's best was not even considered at first; instead, it was placed in another field taking care of sheep—a menial task. You may have been sent out for what seems to be a menial task. I believe this is just a test to see what your attitude is concerning God's appointed timing. Are you being faithful with the sheep (that supposed menial task)? Are you keeping a good attitude when you are out with the sheep? Do you have integrity when you are out with the sheep, accomplishing that "menial task"?

David must have overheard his brothers talking about Samuel's coming. He was on his way to anoint the next king. Even so, David still kept a good attitude taking care of the sheep, which his father had assigned him. But when the time comes, it does not matter if you are taking care of sheep, cleaning toilets, riding on the back of a garbage truck, or working a job that does not pay you what you're worth. When the time comes, the oil will not flow and God will not speak until you are in place—until you come into the room.

So why be upset if there are others before you? Why be jealous? Why have any of those emotions when what God has for you is already set aside? It is for you, and you are the one. You cannot be missed. You cannot be overlooked—not when your time has come—not when the future is in the house. No one will sit or rest until you are in place.

> Are you being faithful with the sheep (that supposed menial task)? Are you keeping a good attitude?

GOD PICKED YOU

God picked you because He gets glory through you. Everybody else can get glory for themselves, but God can get glory through your life. That is why He picked you. God got glory from David's life, and that is why he was the one. Do you want to know why I am the one? Because God can get glory through my life. He can give me wisdom, knowledge, understanding, authority, and power, and I will not lose my mind because I am the one.

You are the one! They did not think you were capable or qualified. They did not think you were adequate. They thought the stuff you did and the things you created were utter foolishness. But the devil is a liar! They did not know you are the one. There is even something creative within you that has not been utilized because they did not know the value of it. But you are the one. There are some things you have not released. They thought you were just scribbling, but you were drawing a map, a blueprint, for success. Do not let anything deter you. The long line is thinning out, and God is ready to release something on your life that has not been released on others. This is the set time, which is why you have to be able to wait in line. It is your turn now. God picked you—you are the one.

PRAYER

Father, we bless, honor You, and thank You for what You do in the lives of Your people. We thank You for scripture that validates Your way of operating. God, You are releasing a word, power, anointing, wisdom, and glory. You are unlocking skill sets and abilities, and breaking chains and shackles off of Your people. God, You are releasing them from the spirit of rejection. Now, others are calling and summoning for them. They are the one. In Jesus' name, Amen.

NOTES

5

I KNEW YOU

"Before I formed you in the womb I knew you; Before you were born I sanctified you; I ordained you a prophet to the nations." Then said I: "Ah, Lord God! Behold, I cannot speak, for I am a youth." But the Lord said to me: "Do not say, 'I am a youth,' For you shall go to all to whom I send you, And whatever I command you, you shall speak."
(Jeremiah 1:5-7)

This scripture is very powerful. Jeremiah was considered one of the major prophets of his day, and he had been pulled aside. God had a special purpose for him, just like He has a special purpose for you. There was a heavenly interaction before there was an earthly conception. God said to Jeremiah, "Before I formed you in the womb"—which was prior to conception, a mother and father coming together—"I knew you." The word *knew* is used as a reference to being intimate or intertwined. God is saying, "We had intimate interaction prior to your parents coming together." Before you were thought of by your mother and your father, you and God knew one another. That is a strong statement! You had communication. You had relations. Before you were born, God sanctified you and set you apart.

1) You were set apart because you are the one.
God set you apart before you were born, not after you were born. This means He had a plan for you from the beginning. You have to realize that He has set you apart because you are the one. I can remember growing up and being around a lot of people, but I did not hang out with large groups because I never felt like I fit. Now, I know the reason for that: before I was born, I was set apart. How could I fit into places that did not cultivate, sharpen, or equip me for my future?

God takes you and sets you apart so that you can identify with what were, in actuality, your relationships in heaven. Now, I know that sounds kind of deep, but it is not. Here's an example: sometimes, I meet a person and the relationship is easy. It seems like it just comes together, even though we've just met. When they walked into the room, I felt like I had known the person for a long time. It is because there was existence prior to conception, and there was a setting apart prior to birth.

I was set apart. God never intended for me to fit into certain groups, so I do not. I'll be nice and cordial, but I am not going to try to fit into something. I have been set apart because I am the one, and you are the one. Hopefully, now you understand that this does not mean there was anything wrong with others. If you are in this process, there is nothing wrong with people simply doing what they do. But when you understand that God knew you, interacted with you, sanctified you, and set you apart, you will stop finding things wrong with others.

I finally realized the reason that others could not handle me: God had set me apart. He did not want me to be the same as everyone else. I have embraced that I am the one. You are the one to get outside of the box. Am I rebellious? Absolutely not. I submit to the structure that God has given me to submit to, and I submit very well. I simply understand that I do not fit into every arena, and this understanding helps me to move further into the destiny that God has for me with confidence.

Knowing that you have been set apart is the source of your confidence. You may go through a season without support or without people who understand you. But now you have an understanding of what that is and what it looks like. You know now that, because you have been set apart, you are the one. And if you are the one, the same process I have gone through may be the process that you will go through. But I can guarantee this: you are going to come out victoriously on the other side. This is not about hurt or the trauma you have experienced. This is about being set apart.

Now, if you try to stay in places even though God has set you apart, you are the one causing the trouble. This was the case with Jonah, who was causing trouble on the ship because he was not where he was supposed to be. There was nothing wrong with the ship. In fact, the ship never would have gone through the storm if Jonah had embraced that he was the one.

Catch this, because this is very important: go ahead and forgive all those people who did not understand you. Now that you are coming to understand yourself and that you have a purpose—now that you understand why and how God maneuvers—do not resist what you know God has set up for you. You know the reason you think differently is because you are different. There is nothing wrong with that.

Knowing that you have been set apart is the source of your confidence.

If I were to sit down with you and walk you through my upbringing, my interactions, my hardships, you would not associate my past traumas with me now, because I do not respond with a traumatic or hurt mindset. Why? I knew that all the things going on—the uneasiness, the challenges—were just an announcement or an alarm going off, indicating that it was time to shift. It was time to move further into what God has for me now.

Let me give another example. If I am going somewhere internationally, I drive to the airport, get out of the car, and go through the airport in order to get on the plane. Depending on where I am going, I cannot simply drive to an international destination. Likewise, there are certain places in your life you have to use one vehicle to reach, and there are others that require another vehicle. When you are the one, you are going to go through these types of transitions. I can travel internationally on a plane or a ship. I'd rather get there sooner on a plane. You choose which vehicle you are going to use, because you are the one.

If you are the one, you have to understand this. There will be transitions. Do not get upset with people. What happened between you was simply an announcement that time's up! You were set apart —you are the one. It is time to move, time to shift.

2) Your immaturity will not cancel God's assignment for your life.
Your immaturity will not cancel God's assignment for your life. What did Jeremiah say?

He told God that he was a youth. That he couldn't even speak! God said, "Do not say that you are a youth." Why? Because God had an assignment for him. Immaturity is trying to stay where God is drawing you out of—the place He's asking you to leave. Immaturity is being in your feelings about something that is actually spiritual—something that is ahead of you. I pray that you get out of your feelings and get into your destiny. Only the immature stay in their feelings.

Jeremiah was going to speak to nations! How in the world can you stay in your feelings and speak to nations? How in the world can you stay in your feelings and do all that God has ordained for you to do? I need you to say or write this again: "I Am the One."

I just took you through the process that must be journeyed by a person who is the one. This journey is from immaturity to maturity, equipping you for purpose. God puts you into certain settings that you do not need to fight, because those settings are getting you ready for purpose. When you are the one, God will put you with people who understand that—people who value your quality. Your immaturity will not cancel God's assignment for your life.

For every Esther, there is a eunuch there to help her get dressed, get prepared, and give her insight about the king. All those things happen when you are the one. Now you know that you are the one, and that all those things that happened were not to destroy you. They were there to push you. When a baby eagle learns how to fly, the mother eagle has to stir up the nest. She even tears up the nest so that the baby eagle gets out and flies. Likewise, in your life, there is a stirring of the nest. Everything is poking you so that you will get out and fly! You do not even realize that you have wings...but you will know soon. You have the ability to fly, to soar, and to do great things because you are the one. I have the ability to fly because I am the one. Thank God that the nest was stirred. Thank God that things started sticking me so that I could not stay in that place. Thank God things were uncomfortable so that I would move on. I am not looking for comfort. I am looking for opportunity. I am looking for destiny, and you are, too. You are the one.

As you read the next section, which is our prayer, begin to let everything go. It was training; it was motivation for where you are going, and now you can see it correctly. All you need to do is get around someone who has wisdom about the journey. When you do this, it will bring ease, keeping you from thinking that the devil is beating you up. No—God is pushing you to where you need to go because you are the one. You are in the right setting.

> # I am not looking for comfort. I am looking for opportunity. I am looking for destiny, and you are, too.

PRAYER

Heavenly Father, thank You for those who are reading this book, whether they be ministers of the gospel, prophets, evangelists, pastors and teachers, or apostles. Whatever field they may operate in, You have not limited them to holding a position in the church. God, You are much broader than that. You created the universe and You would never limit Your people to one small area because You are so vast. You are the beginning and the end. You have the ability to do anything.

God, thank You for causing them to realize that they are the one. You maneuvered and led them certain places in order to bring them to the right place. It was not anything wrong with the people they encountered that caused discomfort; they simply did not realize who they were. They were the ones. Now that they know they are the ones, they are no longer angry, no longer resentful, and no longer in unforgiveness. God, You wanted them to move and realize that there is something greater on the inside of them than what the environment they were operating in had to offer. We thank You that we will no longer try to find peace and comfort in an old place. God, move them speedily from places that are not conducive to what You have placed on the inside of them: these places do not bring vision or sharpen them.

Begin to do some amazing things in their lives that will blow their minds because they are the ones! You are not going to stop nudging them through the power of the Holy Spirit. So therefore, God, if You are not going to leave them alone, they are going to learn how to move with You and embrace saying, "I Am the One." God, put them in settings that will cause them to be stimulated, activated, and to think beyond their present situation. Give them dreams about the morning when they are still in their night season. Give them the ability to believe more in what You said than what may be going on presently. Give them the ability to overcome obstacles and attacks that come from any area.

We thank You that, as You unfold the next level of resources for their lives, they will embrace that they are the ones. No good thing shall be withheld from them; resources are already attracted to their identity—they are the ones. Starting this day, God, bring many creative ideas that they will begin to write down. There will be solutions, because they are the ones. As they begin to type, God, You will fulfill Your purpose through their thought patterns; and when they go back to read what they wrote, they will see that they are not where they used to be. There is a holy release right now—they are no longer hindered, no matter what principalities or powers try to come against them. They will not be held down by any force. They will no longer postpone what You have ordained for now.

I AM THE ONE

"Now faith is the substance of things hoped for, the evidence of things not seen." Father, we decree and declare that it is for right now. Let them begin to see results right now. God, we thank You in advance for a great outcome in the name of our King, Jesus Christ!

NOTES

– 6 –

NO EXCUSES

Then Moses said to the Lord, "O my Lord, I am not eloquent, neither before nor since You have spoken to Your servant; but I am slow of speech and slow of tongue." So the Lord said to him, "Who has made man's mouth? Or who makes the mute, the deaf, the seeing, or the blind? Have not I, the Lord? Now therefore, go, and I will be with your mouth and teach you what you shall say." But he said, "O my Lord, please send by the hand of whomever else You may send." So the anger of the Lord was kindled against Moses, and He said: "Is not Aaron the Levite your brother? I know that he can speak well. And look, he is also coming out to meet you. When he sees you, he will be glad in his heart. Now you shall speak to him and put the words in his mouth. And I will be with your mouth and with his mouth, and I will teach you what you shall do. So he shall be your spokesman to the people. And he himself shall be as a mouth for you, and you shall be to him as God."

(Exodus 4:10-16)

I wanted to be sure that as I wrote and talked about this topic people would understand there's nothing wrong with saying, "I Am the One." Nothing is wrong with saying this; you are not being selfish. To be honest, most of the people who are the one have a hard time processing that they are the one. Moses had a challenge in this passage embracing the fact that he was the one. He gave excuses just like many of us who are called into purpose but run before embracing. So, this book is a tool, a guide to help you to accept and embrace the calling of God on your life. It does not matter whether you are preaching, in government, education, or arts and entertainment, we need you to embrace who you really are—no more excuses.

1) God is aware of your flaws, but you are still the one.
God is aware of your flaws. Let me share this: those who feel like they are less seem to trust God more. I make what I do look very easy. Do you want to know why? Because I started out thinking that I was less, so I trust God more. In fact, I never mount a platform and pick up a microphone without trusting God more. In this passage, Moses is explaining to God that he has a speech impediment—a stuttering problem. He is explaining to God as if God does not know.

Why is it that, when God gets ready for you to do something, you come up with all of these excuses? We point out all these flaws we have as if God does not know. But God chose you because He understood what you had: the problems and even the flaws. He chose you because you are someone who trusts in Him. Jacob wrestled with God and then walked away with a limp. He had to lean on God. I trusted God when I started a ministry with 23 members, and I trust him with 5,000 in multiple locations, because I am leaning on Him. He is looking for somebody who has flaws and realizes they have to trust Him every single day.

> God chose you because He understood what you had: the problems and even the flaws. He chose you because you are someone who trusts in Him.

God is aware of your flaws. They are no surprise to Him. They may be a surprise to the people you are just meeting, but they are not a surprise to God. In fact, God did not fix them because He knew He would be able to use them. The Apostle Paul begins to speak about his weakness. He prayed about this thing three times, and nothing happened. Then God said, "My grace is sufficient for you, for My strength is made perfect in weakness" (2 Corinthians 12:9). God's strength is made perfect in your falls. You may have an anger problem, but the grace of God is coming on you in the area of your anger. Whatever your problems or flaws, God rests on you. It is only when the Spirit of God lifted off of Saul that he was out of control with his anger.

God is resting on you because you said, "I Am the One." Some of you had a quitting problem, but since you are the one, you can no longer quit. Once you realize you are the one and God is not going to send anybody except you, you will do what you need to do with your flaws and insecurities. Here's my thought about the matter: it is not that I am aware of my flaws and weaknesses, but that I am aware of God. I worship Him every day and He is bigger than my flaws. So I'll step out on nothing, because all I can see is something with Him.

2) God is not going to honor your request to send someone other than you.
Moses asks God why He doesn't just send somebody else. After all, Moses has a speech problem. Likewise, we are always telling God to send somebody else. Well, you can talk as long as you want to, but God will not honor that request because you are the one!

I finally came to a place in which I stopped telling God to send somebody else. I am different. I am different from my city, but I am chosen to be where I am right now. I knew I would get backlash. I knew I would get criticism; but I am the one, so it does not matter how much criticism comes. We are built for it. If you are the one, you are built for the criticism and God is not going to get somebody else. Stop trying to judge whether or not you are the one. Stop looking in the closet—there are no skeletons that God does not know about. God needs you to walk in the confidence that He called you to walk in.

You have to embrace the fact that you are the one. The confidence you need will never manifest until you embrace your identity. Nobody is going to be able to do it like you do. Nobody is going to be able to facilitate it like you do. Nobody is going to have the insight that you have. If they get the position, they will not be able to maintain it, because you are the one. That is why I do not get upset if somebody is sitting in my seat—because the seat will not be conducive until I sit in it. Nobody is going to be able to do what you do because God chose you. He kept Moses.

Just look at how He kept everything that was in the "Nile River" from eating you up when you were defenseless. He saw that you made it into Pharaoh's house and that you were raised better than those who came before you. He made sure that you were well-protected. Please excuse me if I am getting preachy…it is not that you made it on your own, but that God was watching over you even as a baby, when you did not know what kind of decisions were being made. Why? Because you are the one.

HE WILL SEND SOMEONE YOU TRUST WITH YOU.

God is not going to honor your request to send someone other than you. You can wait for the rest of your life, or the next ten years—you will just get older. But since you are making excuses, God will send an Aaron with you—someone you trust. He'll give you a staff. What I discovered about entrepreneurs is that they think they have to do everything. Instead, what they should do is surround themselves with the right staff. Some of you are multitasking instead of getting a good staff who will enable you to stay focused while allowing them to be focused on their roles. In this passage of scripture, God tells Moses, in essence, "I am going to give you a staff, not just a rod. I am going to give you your brother Aaron and let him speak on your behalf. You put the words in his mouth, and he'll speak for you." Notice that God also says, "but I am going to put words in your mouth."

So do not say you cannot look for your staff. Look for people who are happy to serve with you. They should not have nasty attitudes, but instead should get excited when it is time to take care of business. Look for your Aaron—those who know they cannot speak unless you speak first! The key to great success is having the proper staff.

1) Because you are the one, you have the responsibility of imparting to those who are assisting you.
Your job is to impart to them. Tell them your dreams and plans. To bring greater clarity to my team, I took at least three Wednesdays to teach on vision with them. What was I doing? I was imparting to those God gave me to see if they were going to rise up and be my support, because I understand that I cannot do everything. My job is to impart to those who are happy about walking with me, not unhappy or disgruntled. I know I am different, but I have to have those around me who will support me being different. In other words, do not try to change for anybody. You are the one. Find somebody who loves who you are and what you are called to do. If you start changing, you will lose yourself and, circumspectly, lose what God purposed for you... and we know how much we need God. So do not change for anybody. Find some people who celebrate who you are, make them your staff, and pay them well.

So Moses had to make an impartation. God told Moses that instead of him speaking, Aaron would be next to him to tolerate his stuttering. God is going to put somebody next to you who can handle your weakness and still honor you. Even though you have a speech impediment, they will still honor you. They will speak for you and not for themselves, honoring that God gave you the word. Every time people get around you because you are the one, you are making an impartation. You have to find people who are not looking at your flaws, because everybody has flaws. Note this: if anybody is constantly looking at your flaws, they have disqualified themselves to be your assistant. Remember, your responsibility is to make an impartation, not do all the work. You make the impartation, and they should go rehearse what you taught them. If not, they are disqualified.

2) You have the heart for the assignment, and others have the skills to assist you.

It is the heart that means everything. A lot of people want to do what you do, but they do not have the heart for it. They will quit easily and walk away. Not everybody is going to stay on a ship that is sinking—but the one that has a heart for the ship will. I love watching the movie "Titanic," especially when the ship is about to sink. When all of the guests and staff are leaving the ship, the captain walks back into the office. He never tried to bail. Anybody who bails from the ship does not have a heart for it and therefore disqualifies themselves from being the captain of the ship. You can always identify the one God sent, because they have a heart for the community and the people.

You can even hear their heart when they open their mouth to speak: they are going to tell you their passion, because from the abundance of the heart, the mouth speaks (Matthew 12:34b). So, if you are the one, you have a heart for the assignment. Others have the skills to assist you. You have to understand the difference between having the heart or having the skills. It is easier to replace skills than heart or passion. You can find a lot of people with skills, but not everyone has a heart. If they do not have a passion, recognize that they simply have skills. Again, we impart to those who have skills, but we never allow skills to rule the organization. You are the one, so it is important for you to figure out who is on your staff or team—those God has called around you who are happy to be with you.

Here's one way to start making that decision: never select people who seem tired when they come around you. The Bible says that Aaron was glad. He walked up with a big smile on his face as he approached Moses. Be careful if people are always frowning when they come around you and think that they are part of your staff. But remember, you are the one: when you surround yourself with the proper people, I believe you are going to have great success.

> **You can always identify the one God sent, because they have a heart for the community and the people.**

3) Because you are the one, you carry the authority to do things that are seen as miracles.
Some people wonder, *Why does the atmosphere shift like that when you get up?* You should boldly say, "Because I Am the One." The atmosphere shifts when you are in your element. If you are a judge, the atmosphere in the courtroom will shift when you arrive. It is not that you asked them to respect you. They do not have a choice but to respect the authority that you walk in because you are the one. Please allow me to impress upon you a level of authority is about to show up—the things you do are going to seem like miracles. Your neighbors are going to wonder, *How did they do that? How did they get that done? How did they shift that? How did they transform?* It looks like miracles from the outside, but you know it is because the Lord is on your side! No weapon formed against you shall be able to prosper (Isaiah 54:17). You run through troops and leap over walls (Psalms 18:29). Let me stress that every time someone speaks against you, it is already condemned; you make happiness look easy. What they fail to see on the outside is that you are the one. They do not know that you paid the price to be happy. You are the one; God is on your side, and all of heaven is cheering for you!

PRAYER

Father, thank You for Your Word and showing us that they are the ones. When it feels like everything around us is falling apart, Lord, thank You for never denying us Your help. When my friends say, "I am all the way out here because You told me," or "I was afraid when You called me, but I stepped out anyway," Lord, help them because they called on Your name. Help them remember that they are the ones. Amen!

NOTES

– 7 –

GOD, I NEED YOUR HELP!

"Now, O Lord my God, You have made Your servant king instead of my father David, but I am a little child; I do not know how to go out or come in. And Your servant is in the midst of Your people whom You have chosen, a great people, too numerous to be numbered or counted. Therefore give to Your servant an understanding heart to judge Your people, that I may discern between good and evil. For who is able to judge this great people of Yours?" The speech pleased the Lord, that Solomon had asked this thing. Then God said to him: "Because you have asked this thing, and have not asked long life for yourself, nor have asked riches for yourself, nor have asked the life of your enemies, but have asked for yourself understanding to discern justice, behold, I have done according to your words; see, I have given you a wise and understanding heart, so that there has not been anyone like you before you, nor shall any like you arise after you. And I have also given you what you have not asked: both riches and honor, so that there shall not be anyone like you among the kings all your days."

(1 Kings 3:7-13)

In this portion of scripture, we see that Solomon is in prayer, carrying on this conversation with the Lord concerning this great people. He asks for something unusual. It is as if, when he asked God for this understanding—this wisdom for how to deal with this great people—it did something in the heart of God. It touched the heart of God deeply.

We observe here that God's heart is always with His people. When you tap into what God is really concerned about, like King Solomon did, you tap into the heart of God concerning people. King Solomon said, "I am not mature enough," and he was being honest. He stated his level of immaturity, much like we do when facing a daunting task. We say things like, "I am not where I need to be; I haven't gone through enough, or attended a university. I don't know how to handle all of this responsibility." Solomon recognized that the responsibility was now on him. God chose him and he was the one. What we see is Solomon's response: *God, I need You to help me!*

Solomon needed God to give him wisdom. When you are the one, you are going to need the wisdom of God—heavenly intervention to help you make judgments about things vast and large. You are going to need God in order to facilitate the increase that He sends into your life—an increase that is beyond your human capacity.

> When you are the one, you are going to need the wisdom of God—heavenly intervention to help you make judgments about things vast and large.

"BUT YOU HAVE ASKED THE RIGHT THING..."

People are everything to God, whether they are good or bad. When you understand this, you will fix your focus on people and ask God for wisdom. He will give you the ability to facilitate people. Solomon said, "I know these people belong to You, so I need Your wisdom for how to deal with them." Now "these" people for you could represent a family—a wife, husband, or children. If you are a pastor, city official, mayor, governor, senator, or president, you are responsible for a community. We need God's wisdom concerning whatever He has given us stewardship over because we are the ones. Now, God understood that we would need Him, but do *you* understand that you need Him? I understand that I need Him, so if you are the one, then you need to understand that too.

ASK FOR THE WISDOM OF GOD

We ask for the wisdom of God concerning what He loves. God loves people. He will look for one among us and call us out. Solomon understands that he is the choice instead of his father, David. He also understands that he is not completely equipped to go in and out amongst the people; they are too numerous; it is too much responsibility, and he needs God's help.

Solomon said, "Therefore give to Your servant an understanding heart to judge Your people, that I may discern between good and evil." In this next season of our lives, we need good judgment concerning people—we need God's help. You have no idea where God is taking you in the next three to six months. I am telling you this: what God has for you is off the radar! At first, you did not believe that God would choose you, but He has. You are the one. Even Solomon, who became the wealthiest man in the entire world—there was none other like him—had to come to the place where he understood that, "I am like a child in the midst of all of this responsibility." God, we need Your help! We make so many decisions in a day, and those decisions have to do with our judgment.

I pose that God is getting you ready. Many things that have been handed to you over a period of time are meant to sharpen your judgment. Can you discern both good and evil? Do you know what is right and what is wrong? How do you deal with vast numbers of people or large responsibilities? You should see this as preparation for greater stewardship, because as God gives more to you, there is more responsibility. But you must know what to ask for, because there are other things that come with correct asking.

A WISE AND UNDERSTANDING HEART

God said to Solomon, "I will give you a wise and understanding heart." Why? Solomon was asking unselfishly. He prayed, in essence, "God, just give me the ability to take care of my people." That is unselfish. It is unselfish when we pray, "Give me the ability to raise my children. Give me the ability to help my community, my church. Give me the ability to take this organization to the next level so that people will enjoy being a part of it." Unselfish asking is what always gets God's attention.

For emphasis, let me say it like this: it cannot be *me, me, me*. It has to be *us, us, us* and *them, them, them*. Catch what I am saying, because you are the one!

I already know what is going to happen for me, but I am more interested in what is going to happen for you. I believe in what is going to happen for me, but I need you to believe in what is going to happen for you. It is going to happen because you are considering others before yourself. You are not asking for long life or riches for yourself. You are not asking that God kill your enemy. In fact, we ask, "Do not kill my enemies—I need enough people to fill the stadium to watch God do great things with my life." Your enemies make up half of the stadium, so they need to see you rise. God is advancing, spreading, and expanding your influence day by day. This is a building-up moment because you are the one. He is encouraging you. This is an edifying moment. All you needed was for someone to start speaking into your life and believing that you would grab ahold of the fact that you are the one. Embrace this fact, and no one can change it. No one has been able to change, talk me out of, or derail me from my assignment. I am the one. We are believing the same for you!

RICHES AND HONOR ARE PART OF YOUR BONUS

According to scripture, because you have not asked selfishly, God is going to give you both riches and honor. No one can stop your wealth or your honor, because you did not ask for that. You asked for a discerning spirit or a judgment to care for God's people. You did not ask for riches or honor, but God says, "I am going to give them to you." This is the bonus for knowing what to ask. Say, "This is my bonus." This is just part of what God does for people who know how to ask for the right thing.

Because of your unselfishness, God chose you. He does not care where you came from or how much He has to mature you. He is willing to make the investment in you because He can trust you with other people. Because God can trust you with people and resources. He will summon you to a certain place. Geographically, God has assigned you to that place with angelic beings to support you in what you do so that you will not fail. I did not say that you would not stumble, but instead that you will not fail. You are not going to fail at your endeavor, but will accomplish everything God has placed in your heart for the advancement of other people. It is going to happen because your concern is not just for yourself, but for the well-being of others.

You are no different than Solomon, who admitted, "I am not adequate enough." God says, "That is okay. You know what to ask for and I know what to give you; and because you have asked for the right thing, I am going to give you more than what you asked for...you are the one."

You are not going to fail at your endeavor, but will accomplish everything God has placed in your heart for the advancement of other people.

PRAYER

Father, thank You for these individuals that You have called for this appointed time. I thank You for the stimulation of their faith. God, thank You for opening up the reservoirs on the inside of them to believe for things that generations before them never obtained. And because they have been processed well, God, You are going to do something so amazing in their lives that has no reference in their bloodlines. They cannot erase the fact that You brought them into this earth for such a time as this, in order to do what nobody else can.

I AM THE ONE

My friend, nobody can do your assignment or withstand the warfare like you can, because you are the one. You are the one who can overcome all adversity. You are the one who can overcome every battle. You are the one who can bounce back from every hit. You are the one who can overcome every tragedy. You are the one, and God has seen you as the one. You have been standing and will continue to stand as God will grace you all the way through. No weapon formed against you shall prosper, and every force that has been working feverishly to discourage you will be put out in the name of Jesus. When you walk into the workplace or get on that Zoom call, you are not going to feel the warfare. It will be depleted and no longer effective in your life. You are no longer going to feel the negativity from those who were trying to discourage you. They will be removed from the room.

Thank You, God, for clarity and focus. We honor You because You are the source and we are Your people. Amen!

NOTES

_____
_____
_____
_____
_____
_____
_____
_____

– 8 –

FIND YOUR INNER STRENGTH

Now David was greatly distressed, for the people spoke of stoning him, because the soul of all the people was grieved, every man for his sons and his daughters. But David strengthened himself in the Lord his God.

(1 Samuel 30:6)

This is an absolutely powerful scripture. It is an account of what was happening in Ziklag. David had taken the army away; when they returned, Ziklag was burned. All the women and children had been taken hostage. David was hurting and in distress, as were those around him. Many times, the account of this particular passage of scripture is preached with the focus on the fact that they recovered everything; but I want to focus on the distress that all of us experience at some point in time. David was *greatly* distressed, not just distressed. He was under acute physical and mental suffering... and as he was going through this moment, he makes a decision.

David faced a really bad situation. His suffering people were grieved beyond grieving, and he was threatened by those he once led. This situation is much like what we have witnessed during the pandemic (COVID-19 and its variants). There has been a lot of grief due to the loss of many lives—loved ones and friends. David was likewise in an extremely distressful situation, but he made a choice to look within and encourage himself in the Lord.

The Lord is within you and His throne is set up inside of you. His throne is your heart, the point from where the Lord functions. If you look at the "I Am the One" logo, you will see a heart in the middle of the flame that is fitted on top of a torch. This symbol represents that you are the one, God is in your heart, and the passions burn from your heart. So David taps into the passions of his heart, and he begins to encourage himself in the Lord. I do not know what you may be facing today, but you need to tap into the passion of your heart and encourage yourself in the Lord.

It is difficult to accomplish great things when you are discouraged, so you have to look deep within yourself. There is a reservoir of encouragement and power there. Oftentimes, people try to figure out how to function. Here's how I function: I look within. No one can ever steal my joy from within. No one can ever steal my peace from within. Everything is stored up within, because His Kingdom is within me. Hence, I am the one. Power and authority are in me. I do not look outside of me. I am not asking my outside circumstances if I can be happy. I am not asking people if I can have joy or peace. Instead, I am going to build myself up on the inside. That is what David began to do. I would like to encourage you to find your inner strength.

> I am not asking my outside circumstances if I can be happy. I am not asking people if I can have joy or peace. Instead, I am going to build myself up on the inside.

1) You have an inner ability to encourage yourself.
God placed in you an inner ability to encourage yourself. So many of you think that you need a certain person or certain thing to happen outside of yourself in order for you to be encouraged. No—you are wired with an inner ability to do this. There have been times when I have been thinking about all of the things that may be going wrong (or not going the way that I know they should) . . . then, all of a sudden, I come to myself and say, "No, I am going to encourage myself in the Lord." I change the screen of what I am seeing in my mind to focus on a lot of good things that are going on presently.

Sure, there may be some things that are not so tasteful going on—maybe even concerning people who are very testing. But, I choose to focus on people who are very supportive, very giving, and very loving. I just changed the screen of what I am going to look at, and I am doing this from within. I am changing the moment, refocusing on something else, and by doing so, I encourage myself in the Lord. So if I am in a battle, I look within and see myself as victorious. I look at what David did when they were in a battle and lost everything, including wives and kids. He changed the screen to victory. He refocused on the recovering of his family and others.

Start seeing the positive instead of the negative and encourage yourself in the Lord. If you do that, you will not need others to encourage you. Inwardly, whether you have a good or a bad day is determined by you. You have an inner ability to encourage yourself in the Lord.

2) When stress has overtaken others, it will not overtake you.
You are the one. You have the ability to strengthen yourself in the Lord and pull strength and comfort from within. When you see people stressing around you, you do not have to join them. People all around David were distressed. He could not find one place where they were not distressed; but when you are the one, you find a way to tap into your inner strength. When others are stressing, you will be the one who has joy, peace, strength, and ability.

I heard this years ago from a Focus Conference by my spiritual father I attended where Dr. Samuel Chand was the speaker. Chand said that, in order to do things on a higher level (like that of my spiritual father), you have to increase your threshold of pain. This means that you cannot internalize everything going on around you. You have to be able to take the blow, and within, still see yourself victorious. When you increase the threshold of your pain, things that are extremely disturbing and depleting to others will not deplete you. It is not because you are not experiencing what they are experiencing; it is because you are the one. You understand that you can tap into your inner strength because of the pain.

I am not talking about becoming numb to pain, but about being able to handle it from within. Because if you are the one, you are a leader, and a leader has to be able to handle pressure without falling apart. So if you can tap into the strength within, you will be the source when everybody is depleted. When you have the inner ability to strengthen yourself, even in the worst moments of your life, you can say you are the one and daylight is coming. When you are the one, you have the ability to stay encouraged in the Lord until the change comes.

3) When you are the one, you can look deep within yourself and find strength.
This is worth repeating. Strength and clarity are not shallow. These things come from deep within, from the core of who you are. God places the quality things within. You never see anything truly expensive on the surface—it is deep at the core. So the darker it gets around me, the deeper I go into the core of who I am, because I am the one. The darker that things become around you, the more you can begin to interact with the part of you that can handle the moment—the inner part of you that can press through the moment and not just survive, but thrive. So in the times when challenging things are happening, you should be thriving, because you are the one.

David began to thrive, and he became more victorious as a leader because of the turbulent time he faced; when he came home and Ziklag was burned, his wives and children were gone, and the whole army was upset. When you are the one, turbulent times are when you thrive the most. Do not let anybody tell you it is time to quit. You are the one who had practice. Do not waste your rehearsals. You can look deep within yourself and find strength.

Allow me to hit this home with you: I found myself in doubtful days, in lonely days. I found myself in days where I felt that I was being betrayed... that is when I found myself. The more the darkness came, the more I looked deep within myself and started to unpack myself. Looking deep within, I started to find the best preacher, the best teacher, the best encourager. I started to find the best articulator of truth. I started to find the wealthy person in me. It was the exterior challenges and turbulence around me that helped me to find the best in me! It was when I could not trust anybody that I went deeper in the Lord, where I found my comfort and trust. If you are in a place where you do not feel like you can trust anyone, look down deep within yourself.

The Bible says in Psalms 121:1-2, "I will lift up my eyes to the hills—from whence comes my help? My help comes from the Lord, who made heaven and earth." Do not look out at a hill, look down within you; that is the hill that God sits on—that which is inside of you. I do not know what you are facing. You may be facing the loss of someone who was very close to you. You may be facing someone who walked out on you. Whatever it is, dig deep, because you are about to pull out the victorious person. You are about to pull out the person who can run through troops and leap over walls. Pull out from your inner strength the greatest entrepreneur that the world has ever known.

I AM THE ONE

In order for you to be great, they have to cut you first. Michael Jordan was one of the greatest basketball players that ever played, and they cut him from the team. But when they cut him, he reached down from within himself and said, "There is a greater person on the inside of me than the one that they cut." See, they cut you because they did not know that you were going to reach within and tap into who you are. When you look within your inner self and see who God has called you to be, you are not just coming back to get what is yours, but what's theirs also. We serve notice to all your enemies that they have lost because you are the one. You are tapping into the corridors of who God created you to be before anything negative ever happened in your life that caused you to have low self-esteem or low self-worth. Say, "I Am the One."

> **It was when I could not trust anybody that I went deeper in the Lord, where I found my comfort and trust.**

PRAYER

Father, we thank You that, as they begin to tap into who they really are, the pressure that has been coming against their lives will no longer make them weak, but strong. It no longer depletes them, but fills them up. It no longer brings them down, but pushes them forward and propels them into the greatest time of their lives.

God, as these people tap from within, let them begin to sing instead of mourn, rejoice instead of being oppressed—until there is an uproar. Because of what You are doing through these people, there will be a sound that is released. Not only will they be free, but their homes, neighborhoods, blocks, and streets will experience freedom. They are the ones. I decree and declare over Your people that, no matter how much they have been looked down on, You see value in them. No matter how much they have been marginalized, You see value in them.

God, You have given them an internal ability to overcome depression, low self-esteem, and low self-worth. They are coming out of the corridors of the damaged places of their past and saying to this world, "Here I am. I Am the One." God, it is settled in the earth and in heaven that they are the ones. They will rule, subdue, and take dominion. Thank You, God, for the identity that You are giving Your people; for the blessing that resonates through their lives; and for the opportunity that You have given this world to have these individuals in the earth in this generation. In the name of Jesus Christ, Amen.

NOTES

_____
_____
_____
_____
_____
_____
_____
_____
_____

– 9 –

GENETICALLY, I AM THE ONE

Now Philip was from Bethsaida, the city of Andrew and Peter. Philip found Nathanael and said to him, "We have found Him of whom Moses in the law, and also the prophets, wrote—Jesus of Nazareth, the son of Joseph." And Nathanael said to him, "Can anything good come out of Nazareth?"
(John 1:44-46)

Genetically, I am the one. I know I am the one, and I know that you are the one. Now, you have to get it down on the inside of you so that it will permeate and be released on the outside. I am going to help you, as you continue to read, to get this fact on the inside of you. This is my job during this season of my life—not to be great, but to make others great. My assignment is to speak a word that will cause the potential in you to rise up to its highest level. I have seen a lot of people, especially at funerals, who did not fulfill their potential while on the earth—but not you. You will not be one of those who, when your time is up, will not have utilized everything God placed in us to subdue, rule, and conquer in the earth. Say this with me: "I Am the One."

There is nothing arrogant about saying this—you are simply tapping into your true identity. Sometimes, you have to talk to yourself, especially in the worst days of your life, and say, "I Am the One." These are not words that you use when you are on the top of the mountain. They are the words you use when you are in the valley, and they solidify the fact that you are going to be back on top of the mountain. I do not know where you are in your life right now, but if you say, "I Am the One," even if you are in your lowest place, get ready for the greatest places!

You are the one. If nobody else recognizes this, know that I recognize it, God recognizes it, and the Holy Spirit on the inside of you recognizes it. As we read, Nazareth was the place where Jesus grew up. I want you to understand that just because you grew up in a certain place or spent some time in a certain place does not mean it is permanent or that it can define you.

1) Where you grew up and what you have been through will not define you. It was an assumption made by Nathanael that goodness could not come from the geographical location of Nazareth. He looked at where they said the goodness was coming from and said, "It cannot come from Nazareth." Somebody may have told you that you cannot be great, or you are not the one, just because of where you grew up—just because you have gone through some trauma in your life, or you were incarcerated and have a record. But this does not mean that you cannot be great. You are still the one. A lot of people wanted to count you out, but they may as well count you in, because nothing about where you came from is going to cancel out where you go. Make an announcement: "This is the day that I am stepping into my purpose."

Assumptions have always blinded individuals from the appearance of goodness. Nathanael's assumptions about Nazareth made him doubt whether or not Jesus could come from there. Whatever you have been through, wherever you are right now, they are making assumptions about you. They are already saying that it will not be possible for you because of where you came from, but this is merely an assumption. Just because they have partial information concerning you does not mean you are not the one. There is no truth to what they said as long as you understand that "Nazareth" cannot hold you back; the ghetto cannot hold you back; drug addiction cannot hold you back; being raised in a single-parent household cannot cancel what God has for you. None of those things can hold you back. You may not even know your biological father, but that cannot hold you back because there is enough in the kingdom of God to establish your identity.

> Just because you grew up in a certain place or spent some time in a certain place does not mean it is permanent or that it can define you.

I came to speak to your identity. There is something inside of you that is going to be released that nobody can stop, because you are the one. Your prophecy is stronger than their assumption. Their assumption comes from their little, limited intellect, but your prophecy came from heaven. Nobody in the earth can erase what God said about you.

2) The word was released in you.
Isaiah 11:1 says, "There shall come forth a Rod from the stem of Jesse, and a Branch shall grow out of his roots." That is a word that says Jesus is coming and there is nothing that can stop it. Generations before He came to earth, it was prophesied.

There is a word about you that was released in the atmosphere. The Bible says, according to Isaiah 55:11, that God's Word "shall not return to Me void." I wrote this book to speak to the word that is on the inside of you— the word that gave you identity. I'm speaking to that word that you put up on the shelf that needs to be pulled back down. I came to speak to that word that is on the inside of you, whether it be that 10-, 15-, or 20-year word.

I am writing to speak to that word that calls you to open your Bible and study like you have never studied before. I came to speak to that word that brought you out of low self-esteem and made sure you did not define yourself by your upbringing. I came to stimulate that word that is already on the inside of you! Shout it in the atmosphere: "I Am the One!" This is not the day you are going to quit, because you know you are the one. Even if you feel like quitting, if you are the one, you know you have to get back in the game. God is calling you by name. You are coming out of that dark place, that low place, that depressed place. The word was released in you, and God wants you out of that place because you are the one.

3) The DNA is stronger than the history of the location.
Nazareth had a reputation for not producing anything good. Nathanael had the assumption that, if Jesus came out of Nazareth, he could not do much. Let me be blunt: I do not care if you live in Lo-debar ("no pasture," "no word," or "no communication"), you are still great. I do not care if you have physical challenges, you are still great. I do not care if you were dropped, you are about to get up. Even Mephibosheth, who had physical challenges, was the one.

When there is somebody who understands the concept David understood when he said, "Is there any left in the House of Saul that I may show the kindness of God to?"—when you are the one—it does not matter how physically challenged you are. I do not care how many times you have been dropped. I do not care what has happened to you. You will hear the sound of somebody sending for you because you are the one.

You have to get your legs together, get your challenges behind you, and walk toward your destiny. It only fits you and it is anointed for you. So stop thinking like a dead dog. Stop thinking like an orphan. Stop thinking like a castaway. Stop thinking like nobody loves you—God loves you. Realize that you are the one and that is why you are still here!

IT IS NOT THE LOCATION—IT IS IN YOUR DNA.

Do you want to know why you made it out? Because it was in your DNA. It is genetic, and that is why you did not come to take sides. It is in your genes to take over.

Let me expound: when you get into a room, you are going to take over; in a neighborhood, you are going to take over; in a classroom, you are going to take over; in the government, you are going to take over; in arts and entertainment, you are going to take over; in fitness, you are going to take over; going into an executive room, you are going to take over; in the hospital, you are going to take over, because you are the one. It is impossible for you to sit there and be quiet when you are the one. Takeover is in your DNA.

It was not in Jesus' location, it was in His DNA. You are the carrier of greatness. Never let anyone change your mind about what God said about you years ago. Even if you feel that your time has passed, you are not too old for this, because you are the one. I do not care how much gray hair you may have—you are the one. I do not care how much muscle you lost—you are still the one. I do not care if you struggle and grunt while getting up—you are still the one. God says you are in your best time, because you are the one.

Now you know how to steward your gift and how to sling rocks at your giants. Now you know how to use your bow and spear because, in the past, you were not sure. Now that you are working through everything you have been through, I came to tell you that this season, there is a bullseye for you. Because you are the one.

1) It is the same today as it was then—the prophetic word will bring it forth.

The prophetic word will bring forth the one for the fulfillment of God's promise. Others thought it would never happen; but now, it is bringing forth the prophetic word that God had already released. You are the one and you are the fulfillment of God's promise. Isaiah 55:11 reads, "So shall My word be that goes forth from My mouth; it shall not return to Me void, but it shall accomplish what I please, and it shall prosper in the thing for which I sent it." So the word over your life cannot fail. Even if you feel like you cannot produce the word on the inside of you, you cannot fail. It will produce forever, because God's Word does not have the ability to return without results. You have a word down on the inside of you that you do not want to lose. So every time you feel like you are getting low or depressed, reach over to your Bible and remind yourself about the great future that you have because you are the one. The Word cannot return void. Even if you are in your 80s or 90s, God's Word has to produce.

We do not quit until His word runs out. Yes, we are still the ones. I am sorry if you want me to quit. I've got too much word over my life to quit. Right now, I've got too much word over my life to go get in a cave and stay there. I've got a command over my life that will not allow me to quit.

Do you know that you are the one? Every person is looking for something. I came to encourage you to not give up until the manifestation of the kingdom of God occurs in your life.

> Even if you feel like you cannot produce the word on the inside of you, you cannot fail. It will produce forever, because God's Word does not have the ability to return without results.

---

2) Unlike people, the word will accomplish the task and bring forth the one.
The word does not have the ability to go out and bring in a vacancy. The word went out that was spoken by the late Apostle Bishop Eddie L. Long concerning Liberia. The word went out and the word continues to work. When you are the one, even in the midst of grieving the loss of a loved one, the word will compel you to go to Liberia. This same word over your life will not let you grieve beyond a certain period of time, because there is work to do and you are the one.

So the word always brings forth. It'll take a Stephen A. Davis from Birmingham, Alabama, and bring him back across the state line and say, "You are not done speaking. There is a sound on the inside of you that the region needs to hear." So I have to keep crossing the state line, because I am the one!

The word of God cannot return void—it reaches over into your situation. You may not have all the answers, and you may not understand everything. Your understanding can wait, but your obedience cannot. The scripture says that God's Word "shall prosper in the thing for which I sent it." The word *prosper* means a state of abundance. There are different meanings, but this is the one I want to focus on: a state of abundance. This is what God is saying to you who are the one, and this is my prayer: "It will be abundantly

I AM THE ONE

seen that you are the one! No one can say it like you say it, and no one can walk in it like you do. If you were bent over, get your back straight—you are the one. We have been saying it, Lord, but now they will see it, in Jesus' name. Amen!"

NOTES

_____
_____
_____
_____
_____
_____
_____
_____
_____
_____
_____
_____
_____
_____
_____
_____
_____
_____
_____
_____
_____

— 10 —

TEST, CONSPIRACY, PRESSURE: YOU ARE THE ONE

And we know that all things work together for good to those who love God, to those who are the called according to His purpose.
(Romans 8:28)

Genesis 50:20 says, "But as for you, you meant evil against me; but God meant it for good, in order to bring it about as it is this day, to save many people alive." The Apostle Paul is writing to the Church of Rome in Romans 8:28, and Genesis 50:20 is the account of Joseph speaking to his brothers who have gone through the process of trying to destroy him. There are several things that happen as you maneuver through Joseph's story. First, they stripped him of his coat. Second, they came up with a strategy of how to kill him. All of a sudden Reuben, the eldest brother, came up with the idea not to kill Joseph, but to sell him into slavery. So thirdly, they sold him into slavery. This course of events, though traumatizing, puts Joseph on the track to the greatness that God spoke over his life in a dream. In this chapter, I am going to dive more deeply into these passages of scripture. We see in both the test, conspiracy, the pressure, and the call.

TEST

In Romans 8:28 we see that, no matter what we are dealing with, whether good or bad, it is working for us. If we consider Joseph's account, his being thrown in the pit and then sold into slavery was working for his good. It was positioning him where God was going to cause him to reign or rule. Even though he was stripped of his coat, thrown into the pit, sold into slavery, falsely accused, and then thrown back into prison, he was still the one. These negative events were working for him and not against him. I like the fact that Joseph did not become resentful, nor did he demonstrate an inner spirit of unforgiveness because of what was happening to him. It was a test.

So in order to get to the place in which he was going to reign, he had to go through these processes, which validates Romans 8:28. Purpose is always inside of the individual who is the one. Please note: If you are the one—and I believe we have established the fact that you are—no matter what season of life you are in, your circumstances are working for you, not against you. Pass the test!

CONSPIRACY

If they desire to kill or destroy you (your reputation) just like they desired to kill or destroy Joseph, someone amongst the pack of the conspiracy will come up with the solution to not take the life—to not completely destroy. Joseph's brothers were all in agreement to kill him until one brother said, "No, let's not do that."

Please catch this: someone amongst your enemies is thinking about helping you get to your destination and they don't even know it! When you are the one, God will maneuver even the people who meant to cause you harm to be working for your good. You were not completely destroyed, so God had a plan for you. If you are reading this today, every conspiracy that was against you contained somebody working for you, because God would not allow the entire team to destroy you.

You may feel like this is just too much. No, it is not too much! There is always something God is doing to make sure that His investment in you is not wasted. God is not going to let anyone or anything destroy you, because you have purpose in you.

> No matter what season of life you
> are in, your circumstances are
> working for you, not against you.

---

1) You are the one, so do not worry about the conspiracy.
The original plan will not be fulfilled if it is working against the purpose of God that is in you. You are going to be able to say what Joseph said in Genesis 50:20: "But as for you, you meant evil against me; but God meant it for good, in order to bring it about as it is this day, to save many people alive." God was maneuvering things the entire time.

Many times, people around you think they are in control. No, God is still in control. He is like the boundaries or guardrails to what is going on in your life. If it seems to be negative, there are guardrails. The negativity can only go so far. I have lived long enough to know that there are guardrails on each side of me. My enemy may not see them, my opposers may not see them, but I know they are there. Others may cause me to swerve, but they cannot run me off the highway. It is the same with you. Circumstances and opposition can cause you to swerve, but they cannot drive you off the highway. Why? Because you are the one! You are on the highway to the destiny God created for you. Therefore, anything that tries to derail you cannot, because there are guardrails.

In Joseph's life, every situation was leading him where God wanted to take him. Every opposition was leading him to that place. He was the one, which is why he told his father, mother, and brothers his dream. What he was telling them was, "I Am the One." There were guardrails leading him all the time on the highway to his destiny. What if Joseph had stayed with his father, who favored him? He never would have been in place to save many lives.

Do not get disappointed. There will be—and I am sure there have already been—some distasteful things that have happened in your life. But those things that were meant for evil, God used to put you right in that fine line where He wants to take you. This is how God operates. Any time things seem to be delayed, things are right in the timing of God. So never consider a delay a denial. A delay puts you right in the timeline of God.

This is what I do if something is not happening in the time in which I wanted it to happen: I tell myself that God did not want that to happen right now, according to my timeline. If it had, it may not have been as profitable to me or to others. So if that timeline is never too late with God, it is never too late for us! You may be getting ahead of yourself. If you get that thing too soon, meet that person too early, arrive before the doors open... delays can be very discouraging, but you are in the timeline of God.

I used to wonder why certain things did not happen. I would say, "We could have done this, Lord, some years ago." However, God revealed to me that we were right on time. I am the one. I am the right age, the right color, living in the right neighborhood, operating under the right influence. I am in the right timeline and right where God wants me. I am moving in what God wants me to move in. I am thinking the way God wants me to think, and I am not on pause. I am moving, things are happening, and I am right where He wants me to be. He prepared me to be the one.

> **Never consider a delay a denial. A delay puts you right in the timeline of God.**

You also have to see everything that you have been processing as preparation. Everything has been preparing you for this day, because you are the one. Now let me share this revelation: if your enemy had known this fact, he never would have tried those things. If he had known that they were simply your preparation, he never would have gone to that extent to equip you. The opposition prepared you for the moment in which God is going to use you greatly, because you are the one. What God does not stop, He will use.

2) You will never be destroyed by the pressure.
You may feel like things are trying to destroy you, but they are not. You will never be destroyed by the pressure. The pressure is bringing some things out of you, but it is not going to destroy you...we can see the growth you've undergone from your trial.

3) We can see your growth from your trial: you are called.
We can see in your eyes: you are more powerful now. You are more experienced. You have more wisdom. You may not think about it, but we see it. Oftentimes, others are more aware of the changes happening within us than we are.

Others can see your growth and maturity. They can see you functioning in something that you were not functioning in a year ago. They can see how you are evolving and moving forward. They can see that you are the one now. You have to start embracing the fact that the trial made you—you were growing through that trial. If you want to be great, keep allowing the pressure and trials to evolve you. Let them gift you with a consistent prayer life and transform you into a critical thinker.

I am a thinker and prayer is my lifestyle, so I am going to think my way through. I am going to come up with a solution. And guess what? When I come up with that solution, I am going to lead everybody out. I figured out in the midst of my trial that I was the one. Now, I am telling you that, even during the midst of trials, *you* are the one, as well. If you have not written it, go ahead and write it now.

I want to remind you of Genesis 50:20: "But as for you, you meant evil against me; but God meant it for good, in order to bring it about as it is this day, to save many people alive." Joseph went through many trials and became the savior of his father, his brothers, and many people alive. He went through the test, the conspiracy, the pressure, and found that he was the one. So it is with you: you are the one surviving every test and trial; you are the one moving through in spite of the conspiracy; you are the one standing under the pressure; and you are the one who will make it big. This is absolutely phenomenal. We are going to speak into your life through prayer and let God do what He always does!

PRAYER

Father, as we conclude this chapter, we honor You. God, You are moving on their behalf, because they are the one. There is no pressure that can come their way that they cannot survive. It is not breaking them—it is making them. It is forging them into what You would have them to be. God, they are becoming a resource to the world, not just to their household.

The pressure is bringing ideas and strategies out of them that they never would have had otherwise. They are becoming more compassionate towards others because of what they are experiencing now. Rather than finding wisdom, they are studying, God, so that they can bring resolve to many people's lives. They are becoming a rescuer to those who need to be rescued because there was no one to rescue them. Father, they are becoming counselors to those who need counseling because no one was there to counsel them. They found a way to make it through.

Father, continue to exceed the boundaries of what people thought about them. They are the solution to their neighborhoods. They are the solution to their bloodlines. They are the solution to this nation and to this world because of the pressure that they have survived. Father, we do not ask that You remove the experience—we ask that You use the experience. God, maybe they were born in a dysfunctional household and that You gave them a passion to create functional homes all around the world. Whatever it is, do not let them live in the hurt of their past, but let them be a solution because of what they have experienced.

God, I decree and declare over every life that has experienced any traumatizing moments that the things that tried to delay and haunt them will no longer haunt them. God, You are maneuvering in their lives and bringing them up for such a time as this. You created passion inside of them that nothing can stop or extinguish. They will not revisit the past as pain but as a solution. They will see and detect those who are close to them who have experienced what they have experienced, and use their own insight to bring them out. They will use those years of depression, God, to bring others out of depression.

God, for any person who has suffered without resources, now they know who Jehovah Jireh is and they are bringing the spirit of Jehovah Jireh, "The Lord Who Provides," into the room. They will cause others to believe that they too can have the resources needed to live a full life. Those who have been traumatized in secret will be able to pick up on the little girls and boys who are suffering and will be their answer because they are the one. They will create institutions and programs that will cause people to do great things.

They have endured pressure, but it could not destroy them. God, create in them a heart for areas where they can use their past pain as a solution. Let there be fathers and mothers who have a heart for children who have been traumatized simply because they went through it but were not destroyed by it. Father, thank You that the spirit of suicide could not have them because Your purpose is all over them. The suicidal spirit did not destroy them, and because it did not destroy them, God, now they have become the answer. Now they are understanding that the traumatizing moments which did not destroy them made them. Father, let them begin to rise up because they are the one and have processed well everything they have been through. God, they have stepped on the platform of performance to bring glory to heaven.

You are now on that platform. You are now the tool that God is going to use to transform regions. You are now there. You are at that place. Yes, you have been through, but you made it. Yes, it was tough, but you made it. Yes, it was pressure, but you made it. And now that you have made it, we are going to activate your experience so that everywhere you go, you are going to be a blessing to people. You understand what it feels like: the sleepless nights, the tears running down your face. Now that you understand, and now that you are being activated—now that you are moving into the place God has ordained for you—the trauma is no longer effective. Instead, you deliver those who are in trauma. And even if you are still having moments, God says, "I am going to use you even though you are still in a catastrophic moment, because you have the right perspective."

I believe that the Spirit of God is coming on you. I believe that the wisdom of God is coming on you, just like it did with Joseph before he became the governor. He was in jail and yet he was still encouraging and giving revelations of dreams and visions. You will be able to do it because you are the one. Nothing you have gone through has dampened you. No, I believe that you have become sharper, better, and more discerning through the process. Now you are ready!

Father, thank You for Your blessings, for Your anointing, and for reserving Your people for such a time as this. You called them and You compel them to say, "I Am the One." Amen.

NOTES

_____
_____
_____
_____
_____
_____
_____

– 11 –

I AM

But Moses said to God, "Who am I that I should go to Pharaoh, and that I should bring the children of Israel out of Egypt?" So He said, "I will certainly be with you. And this shall be a sign to you that I have sent you: When you have brought the people out of Egypt, you shall serve God on this mountain." Then Moses said to God, "Indeed, when I come to the children of Israel and say to them, 'The God of your fathers has sent me to you,' and they say to me, 'What is His name?' what shall I say to them?" And God said to Moses, "I AM WHO I AM." And He said, "Thus you shall say to the children of Israel, 'I AM has sent me to you.'"

(Exodus 3:11-14)

As you read this scripture, I am going to give you adequate information to believe in the shirt ("I Am the One") that many people—and hopefully you—are wearing. This chapter is entitled, "I AM." I AM means for every need, I AM; every need that you have, that "I AM" on your shirt has the ability to meet. In this passage of scripture, as Moses is asking God, "Whom shall I say sent me?" God said, "Tell My people . . ." He wasn't talking about Egypt, but about the people of Israel.

"I AM Who I AM" is translated as, "I will be who I will be." I do not know what you need Him to be today, but there are 365 names of God in the Bible. There are 365 days in the year, and He has a name for every day. Let's think on this! For every situation, God has a name. For every attack, He has a name. There are 365 names for God... Now, there is a tendency, if you are not a person who studies the Bible and history, to say that the "I Am the One" T-shirt is about Stephen A. Davis. There may be a tendency to think in this manner, which simply denotes that these thoughts are formed from ignorance or from being unlearned. The basis of this chapter is to solidify the fact that when you see the I AM, it is a statement saying that God orchestrated it, not me. He just needs you to wear it!

What does this mean, to *wear it?* God was always interested in placing His name on His people. Numbers 6:22-27 states this:

> And the Lord spoke to Moses, saying: "Speak to Aaron and his sons, saying, 'This is the way you shall bless the children of Israel.

> *Say to them: "The Lord bless you and keep you; The Lord make His face shine upon you, and be gracious to you; the Lord lift up His countenance upon you, and give you peace;" So they shall put My name on the children of Israel, and I will bless them."*

God is always interested in writing His name on you. Sometimes, you just have to "put" it on (wear your "I Am the One" T-shirt); sometimes, you may have to "drink" it (from the "I Am the One" water bottle); sometimes, you may need an umbrella when it is raining (shelter under the umbrella named, "I Am the One"). Regardless, His name is everything we need.

Again, my purpose for writing this chapter is to bring greater understanding about the statement "I Am the One." This is not a promotion or some tool we are using to raise money. No, it is something we are saying from heaven. When the devil sees God's name on you, he knows what it means—even when other people don't. The devil knows that, when the name "I AM" is on us, something is going to open up and work for our good!

There are some who may want to leave the name "I AM" in the Old Testament, but it is also found in the New Testament. We understand the Hebrew name of God in the Old Testament as I AM. This name also means Yahweh. God has names to define Himself for what He is going to do for His people. There is a name for every problem that you have today. For those who need healing, He is Jehovah Rapha. For those who are lonely, He is Jehovah Shammah (He is there, present with you). But when you say, "I AM," He is all of that. Even if you do not know Jehovah Rapha and you need to be healed, just say, "I AM." If you need His presence or are feeling lonely, just say, "I AM."

In the Old Testament, because the true gospel was constantly under attack, God's name had to be represented in symbolism. There was war against God's Name and all that I AM represented. Bringing this symbolism forward into our present day, when others tell you that you cannot pray in school, we must have symbolism to keep I AM in the school system. Likewise, to keep I AM in the neighborhood, or on the job, there has to be something representing it so those who created the laws against it do not know the symbolism. When you have a principal who carries "I AM" on the inside (even wearing the T-shirt, "I Am the One"), he or she is symbolic of the "I AM" in the school. When you go to your job, God is represented there through you. I AM is wherever you go. You are the symbolism that God exists in that place. How can they lock God out and let you in? It is not possible to lock God out, because you are the symbolism that God still exists. He exists in you. Remember, you are the one!

God has names to define Himself for what He is going to do for His people. There is a name for every problem that you have today.

In John 8:58, Jesus said to them, "Most assuredly, I say to you, before Abraham was, I AM." They were discussing that Jesus was not even 50 years old—how could He say that He knew Abraham? Jesus is saying, as He says in other portions of scripture, "I AM everything. I am the Alpha—I was back then, in the beginning—and I am the Omega—I AM the end. I AM is always here." In other words, you cannot eliminate I AM. He is all the way back in the book of Genesis and all the way forward in the book of Revelation; from generation to generation, they will never be able to get I

AM out. So why are you concerned about where you feel like God is not? He is still there. I AM is still there.

John 18:4-6 says, "Jesus therefore, knowing all things that would come upon Him, went forward and said to them, 'Whom are you seeking?' They answered Him, 'Jesus of Nazareth.' Jesus said to them, 'I am He.' And Judas, who betrayed Him, also stood with them. Now when He said to them, 'I am He,' they drew back and fell to the ground." Why? Because anytime "I AM" shows up, all of your enemies have to bow. It did not say that Jesus did not have enemies, but that they could not arrest Him before they bowed before Him. Have you ever watched the TV show "Cops"? Have you ever seen the police officers bow down to the perpetrator before making the arrest? No! But before the Roman soldiers could even arrest Jesus, they had to bow down, paying homage and respect to Him. Likewise, before anyone can do anything to you, they will have to bow before you, because I AM is in you.

These were Roman soldiers. They were very well-equipped. They were well-trained, but they had to bow because I AM spoke. I believe today, I AM is going to speak so loudly through you that everything that has been in opposition to you must bow. It does not matter if it is cancer, diabetes, or mental illness—they all must bow to I AM! I want you to understand the empowerment of the T-shirt, "I Am the One." Receive and know that, from this day forward, everything that has worked against your life no longer gains success over you. Allow me to share more about why we are empowered.

BECAUSE GOD (ELOHIM) IS THE ONE, I AM THE ONE.

You cannot tell me I am not the one. I get my identity from Him being the one. That is why God said to Moses, "Tell them I AM sent you."

Because if I AM, you are. So if I AM sent you, I AM is with you. Elohim is another name for the Old Testament God of Israel. This particular name lets you know that I AM is the head of it all. So to all of our religious skeptics who are thinking we have drifted away, no—we have drifted right into place. Notice that, on the T-shirt, the words "I AM" are larger than the words "the One." I did not tell my graphic designer to enlarge the words "I AM"—it was the Spirit of God flowing and the assignment that was given. God has a way of working even through graphics, and He'll work through you to make sure He is magnified in the midst of His people.

After a pandemic, after a catastrophic event has touched this globe, we need something more than a little slogan. We need something to help us. We survived it, but we are traumatized. Because of all the things we have been through, we are still a little nervous when we go out in public. We need something greater than the trauma we have been through, and I suggest that I AM is the one. I believe I AM is able to get you through anything.

After 430 years, I AM, the God of the children of Israel, brought them out of bondage. He caused Pharaoh and Egypt to become bankrupt. God's people came out of captivity with all the wealth. I believe God is transferring some wealth, because wealth has to move where I AM is going. Are you ready for money that you did not sign up for? I believe the reason that David had so much success over the Philistine giant was because I AM was with him. Here's a good lesson people should remember: never mess with someone who loves to praise God, the I AM. Their praise is a sign that they have a Deliverer who will fight for them—so leave them alone.

THE TERM "I AM" CARRIES THE FULL EXPRESSION OF GOD'S POWER FOR EARTHLY DEMONSTRATIONS.

Pharaoh did not know what was happening after Moses came off of Mount Sinai. He thought he was dealing with the same Moses that he grew up with, but this Moses went and had a conversation with I AM. So, when he came back from Mount Sinai, not only did he come as Moses, but he also came wearing I AM. I believe that, as you are reading this book, you are going up higher. You are having a conversation not with just a person, but with I AM; and when you come back down, your face is going to be shining. When God gets ready to use you as a deliverer, I AM will sit down on the inside of you. I AM is the full expression of God's power for earthly demonstrations. If you do not have an earthly demonstration, most people will not believe in I AM. But I AM will be with you to bring deliverance.

> Whether it is three or four o'clock in the morning, in the afternoon, or late at night, He responds to His name. He is the Great I AM!

As I started to think about how "I AM" carries the full expression of God's power for earthly demonstrations, I thought about what some churches use as an earthly demonstration. I'm not merely trying to sell a t-shirt; I came out of churches where people would pray over pieces of cloth before placing them inside the pillows, garments, or shoes of the person for whom they were praying. Now, this same principle still works: all we have to do is put a T-shirt on that alcoholic, on that drug addict, or on that troubled child. Once I AM gets a hold of them, all of a sudden, their character will begin to change. So every time we say, "I Am the One," the One who is the

"I AM" responds. Do you think you can say, "I Am the One," without God responding? God knows what His name is and will respond. God moves based on His name, so every time you say, "I Am the One," God shows up.

You may be thinking, "I thought we had to say Jesus or Jehovah." Yes, we do; but God knows His name also as "I AM." When it is time for a great deliverance—time to get our young Black men off the streets, stop them from committing murder; when it is time to save a race of people that are internally destroying themselves—what we need is I AM to show up in the midst of His people. So when we start saying "I AM," every race, whether Black, Hispanic, White, or Asian, responds to His name.

Say, "I Am the One." You can call other people and they may not respond, but when you call His name, "I AM" always responds. Even when you are having the worst day of your life, look in the mirror with your "I Am the One" T-shirt on and say, "I Am the One"! All of a sudden, an inner courage and excitement will enter your life. Not only did you say what was on the T-shirt, but you said His name, and He responds to His name—whether it is three or four o'clock in the morning, in the afternoon, or late at night, He responds to His name. He is the Great I AM!

I AM DENOTES SELF-IDENTITY AND SELF-SUFFICIENCY.

When people leave you, you can tell them that they were not your source anyway! You must become stable when people walk away from you; only people who don't know who they are will fall apart. But when you know who you are, you realize that others are not your sustenance. You must realize that you existed before they came into your life and you will exist afterwards. Self-identity says, "You do not define who I am; that has already been done by The I AM."

When I wear my "I Am the One" T-shirt, it signifies that I do not have to perform for others in order for them to stay with me, because I'm performing for the Great I AM. And if He has already embraced me, then things are always going to get better, no matter who leaves me.

Now, let's talk about being self-sustained or self-sufficient. There was a certain process in choosing leadership for the 12 Israelite tribes: they took a branch from each tribe and cut it off from its source. Then they all placed their branches into the Ark of the Covenant. The next day when they returned, one rod had budded. It was cut off from the source, yet it was still productive. You can always tell when I AM is with you. You can lose a job and open a business. Someone may decide to leave you, but you are able to buy the house you thought you could not afford without them. Self-sufficiency says, "You may leave me, but I'm going up, not down." Things will get better if I AM is with you. I do not care how horrific the thing that you have gone through—it is getting better. You may have thought, "I'll never be able to get over this." No, you will! I AM is with you, and you will get over that hurdle—whatever it is, you are *already* over it. In fact, you are looking back at what you were trying to get over! You are wearing more than a t-shirt; you have power written across your chest that states, "I Am the One." Anytime you say, "I Am the One," God responds to His name.

WE CAN NEVER USE THE TERM "I AM" WITHOUT GETTING GOD'S ATTENTION, BECAUSE IT IS HIS NAME.

God does not have the ability to turn a deaf ear to His name. That is why it is important not to get quiet when you are in trouble. On your worst days, say, "I Am the One." When it is not going right, say, "I Am the One." When everything is falling apart, "I Am the One." When the money is looking funny, "I Am the One."

Religion tells us that we are no longer putting God first, but only because they put Him last. They tend to say to us that, because we are wearing "I Am the One" T-shirts, we are not putting God first. On the contrary, this is what happens when we say, "I Am the One": we are calling His name first. We are saying that Jesus is the ONE. The Greater One lives within me (1 John 4:4). He is riding in my car, which means He is doing what I could not do without Him. Religious-minded folk tend to say that we are misappropriating the name of the Lord. What they did not study is the 365 names of God. They do not know that there is power in every name. There is no name of God that is depleted of power. In 25 years, I have never been able to produce as much unity as we are producing with "I Am the One." Unless you point the people to I AM, you will never have the level of unity amongst the people of God that you should.

THE KEY TO RELIEVING THOSE WHO HAVE BEEN OPPRESSED IS ANNOUNCING THAT I AM THE ONE IS PRESENT.

Whenever you come amongst a people who have been oppressed, the announcement is what God told Moses: "Tell the people that I AM sent you." The Israelites had spent 430 years in oppression. Any time people have experienced long-term oppression, you have to bring forth the phrase "I Am the One." After 430 years of bondage, it is time to go free. My announcement to you is that, after however many years you have been oppressed, today you go free. I came to make an announcement that I AM is here, and that means you go free—financially, socially, and mentally. Regardless of the conditions, you are still the one; do not have an identity crisis, regardless of what you have been through. The reason people will try to remind you of your past is because they are afraid of your future. There are some people who are afraid that you will have your identity established and that you will be self-sufficient; then you will not have to depend on them to call and pray for you. You can pray for yourself and get the breakthrough!

I AM THE ONE WILL BE THE MOST LIBERATING MOVEMENT FOR MILLIONS OF OPPRESSED PEOPLE AROUND THE WORLD.

Say, "We are just getting started." You are not going to be able to go to the grocery store, the mall, or even travel out of town without seeing "I Am the One." Yes, you are going to see the names of God everywhere you go; you may even see some of us in the casino. We tend to take over! We are going to be everywhere; you may be looking around in the club saying, "It is one o'clock in the morning—what are you doing in here?"

I Am the One. I Am the One who is the president of this company. I Am the One who is the CEO. I Am the One. This is more than a T-shirt. This is more than a catchphrase. Let everybody know that you are the one—you are chosen by God. Now, continue to say . . . I Am the One.

NOTES

_____
_____
_____
_____
_____
_____
_____

www.ingramcontent.com/pod-product-compliance
Lightning Source LLC
Chambersburg PA
CBHW062116080426
42734CB00012B/2883